THE OLYMPICS
SCANDALS

THE OLYMPICS
SCANDALS

Moira Butterfield

SEA-TO-SEA

Mankato Collingwood London

This edition first published in 2012 by

Sea-to-Sea Publications
Distributed by Black Rabbit Books
P.O. Box 3263, Mankato, Minnesota 56002

Printed in the United States of America, North Mankato, MN.

9 8 7 6 5 4 3 2

Published by arrangement with the Watts
Publishing Group Ltd, London.

Library of Congress Cataloging-in-Publication Data

Butterfield, Moira, 1960-
  The Olympics: Scandals / by Moira Butterfield.
      p. cm. -- (The Olympics)
  Includes index.
  ISBN 978-1-59771-320-7 (library binding)
  1. Olympics--Juvenile literature. 2. Sports--Corrupt practices--Juvenile literature. I. Title.
  GV721.3.B88 2012
  796.48--dc22
                                   2011006473

Series editor: Sarah Ridley
Editor in chief: John C. Miles
Designer: Jason Billin
Art director: Jonathan Hair
Picture research: Diana Morris

Picture credits: Alinari/Topfoto: 20b. Vincent Almavy/AFP/Getty Images: 25c.
AP/Topham: 3,15. Giuliano Bevilacqua/Rex Features: 7. Russell Cheyne/Getty Images:
19b. Tony Duffy/Getty Images: 23. Eastlight/Rex Features: 29t. Mary Evans PL: 14b.
Romeo Gacad/AFP/Getty Images: front cover, 22. Imagno/Austrian Archives/Topfoto:
10t. Richard Lam/Rex Features: 21t. Christopher Lee/Getty Images: 19t. Metropolitan
Museum of Art, NY/Topfoto: 8b. A d'agli Orti /Getty Images: 9. PA/Topham: 25t.
Picturepoint/Topham: 10b, 11t, 11b, 24. Rex Features: 29b. RIA-Novosti/Topfoto: 5, 18.
Roger-Viollet/Topfoto: 12. Jewel Samad/AFP/Getty Images: 17. Sipa Press/Rex Features:
8t, 13, 28. Time Life Pictures/Getty Images: 16. Topfoto: 6, 14t, 27cl, 27cr. Ullstein
bild/Topfoto: 20c, 26.

*Every attempt has been made to clear copyright. Should there be any inadvertent omission
please apply to the publisher for rectification.*

April 2011
RD/6000006415/002.

Note to parents and teachers

Every effort has been made by the Publishers to ensure that the web sites in this book
are suitable for children, that they are of the highest educational value, and that they
contain no inappropriate or offensive material. However, because of the nature of the
Internet, it is impossible to guarantee that the contents of these sites will not be altered.
We strongly advise that Internet access is supervised by a responsible adult.

CONTENTS

THE OLYMPICS

The original Olympic Games were held in ancient Greece every four years. The Games were revived in 1896 and are now the biggest sports and TV event on the planet.

The modern Olympics include the Summer and Winter Olympics, the Paralympics, and the Youth Olympics. The International Olympic Committee (the IOC) is in charge, made up of members from different countries.

Sticking to the Rules

The IOC has a strict set of rules, called the Olympic Charter, regarding the organization of the Games. At the beginning of each Games one competitor repeats an oath on behalf of every athlete taking part, promising to abide by the rules:

"In the name of all competitors, I promise that we shall take part in these Olympic Games, respecting and abiding by the rules that govern them, in the true spirit of sportsmanship, for the glory of sports and the honor of our teams."

▶ French athlete George Andres takes the Olympic oath in Paris in 1924 in this artificially colored photo.

The Olympic Creed

There is also an official Olympic Creed, which explains the ideals behind the Games:

"The most important thing in the Olympic Games is not to win but to take part, just as the most important thing in life is not the triumph, but the struggle. The essential thing is not to have conquered, but to have fought well."

Olympic Troubles and Triumphs

The Olympics have produced some of the most amazing achievements in sports ever but they have also been connected with cheating scandals, political protests, and violence. This book is a record of the scandals and the cheating that has come to light in different Olympic Games alongside the many sports triumphs.

The Olympic Flag has five rings representing the five continents of the world from which the athletes are drawn.

Amazing Olympics

In 1924, the IOC introduced the Olympic motto: *Citius, Altius, Fortius.* Translated from Latin this means: Higher, Faster, Stronger.

Olympic Facts and Stats

2008 At the Beijing Games, more than 11,000 athletes from 204 countries took part.

2008 At the Beijing Paralympics, more than 4,200 athletes from 148 countries took part.

2008 The Beijing Games drew the biggest TV audience ever, with an estimated 4.7 billion viewers.

2010 At the Vancouver Winter Games, more than 2,600 athletes from 82 countries took part.

ANCIENT TROUBLE

The first Olympic Games on record took place in 776 B.C.E. at Olympia in ancient Greece. Like the modern Olympics, the ancient Games attracted large crowds. They also had their share of cheaters and arguments.

Ancient Greece was divided into separate city-states and each athlete represented their own home city-state (called a *polis*). City-states that were at war with one another were supposed to have a month-long truce to allow athletes and crowds to travel safely to Olympia. The city-state of Sparta was banned from the Games in 420 B.C.E. when it broke the truce and attacked a neighbor. When a Spartan named Lichas entered his chariot horse team anyway, and won, he was caught and whipped.

Wrestling was an event at the ancient Greek Games, and is still an Olympic sport.

No Women Allowed

A crowd of up to 40,000 watched the ancient Games from a specially built stadium, but married women were banned from attending. If they were caught, they could be punished by being thrown off a high cliff to their death. There is only one record of a married woman being caught, though

Olympic athletes shown on an ancient vase. The athletes ran naked.

Olympic Facts and Stats

The judges were people from the local area around Olympia. They were considered more trustworthy than people from other parts of Greece.

Breaking an opponent's fingers was allowed in the wrestling event, but not biting or grabbing someone's genitals.

332 B.C.E. The city of Athens boycotted the Games in protest at one of their athletes being punished. He had bribed his opponents to lose.

67 C.E. Roman Emperor Nero took part in the Olympics and was declared the winner of everything he entered.

not killed. She was an athlete's mother who disguised herself as a male trainer. Perhaps because of her, the judges brought in a new rule that all trainers at the Olympics, like the athletes, had to be naked.

Cheating and Bribes

Athletes swore on a slice of boar's meat that they wouldn't take bribes or cheat. If an athlete was found cheating, he was disqualified, whipped, and made to pay a fine. The money was used to make a bronze statue of Zeus, displayed at Olympia with the cheater's name carved on it. Sometimes rival city-states bribed the best athletes to switch teams. For instance, Astylos of Kroton won six Olympic races for his home city but was then bribed to run for the rival city of Syracuse. The angry people of Kroton pulled down the statue of him back at home and destroyed his house.

A bronze statue of Zeus, the ancient Greek god to whom the Olympics were dedicated.

Amazing Olympics

Eventually, the Games were banned in 393 C.E. by Roman Emperor Theodosius, who was a Christian and thought the Olympics were too pagan.

NEW GAMES, NEW PROBLEMS

🔵 Baron de Coubertin
(1863–1937)

In the 1880s, a French nobleman named Baron Pierre de Coubertin decided to revive the idea of the Olympic Games. Some of these early Games did not go smoothly, and the whole idea was very nearly abandoned.

The first modern Olympics took place in Athens, Greece, in 1896. It was a small event with only men taking part—mostly Greeks or people on vacation in the country at the time. According to a British competitor, George Stuart Robertson:

"There wasn't any prancing about with banners and nonsense like that…it was all a splendid lark."

Troubled Times

The next few Olympics were very disorganized, taking place over many months instead of a few days, and with no proper ceremonies or rules. There were lots of arguments, for example, over whether athletes should race on a Sunday and whether they should be paid. The IOC insisted that all Olympic competitors

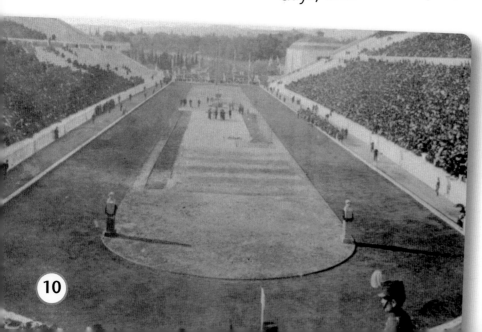

🔵 The stadium built for the 1896 Olympics was a reconstruction of one originally built in 330 B.C.E.

should be amateurs, earning no money from sports. This made it difficult for people who were not wealthy to compete, although some were supported by patrons.

Rules for Women

At the first modern Olympics there were no women competitors. Women athletes first appeared in 1900 but not in track and field events or gymnastics until 1928. When several female athletes collapsed in the 800-meter race in 1928, this led to a ban on women competing in an Olympic race longer than 200 meters. The ban lasted until 1960.

Felix Carvajal runs in the 1904 Olympics, when all athletes had to be amateur.

Amazing Olympics

Ski jumping for women is still not a Winter Olympic event. As recently as 2005, it was said to be "not appropriate for women from a medical point of view."

Charlotte Cooper of Great Britain, the first female Olympic champion. She won the women's tennis in 1900.

Olympic Facts and Stats

1900 The Paris Games were so badly organized that some athletes didn't even realize they were in the Olympics at all.

1900 A French croquet team were the first women to compete in the modern Olympics.

1908 At the London Games, the marathon was made more than a mile longer than normal to start outside Windsor Castle so that the royal children could watch from inside.

MONEY VS. LOVE

For many decades the IOC maintained that every Olympic athlete had to be amateur, not earning money from sports. Over the years this led to many competitors being banned or stripped of their medals for breaking the rules.

The amateur rule was inspired by two ideas. One was the mistaken belief that athletes at the ancient Olympics were not given financial support. The other developed in nineteenth-century England, with the idea that sports were good for the mind and body but that it was very ungentlemanly to want to win too badly or to earn money from sports. This idea also had the effect of ensuring wealthy athletes did not have to compete against those from poorer backgrounds, who would find it difficult to give their time without pay or prize money.

No Wages Allowed

Athletes were banned from the Olympics if they had ever earned any money from sports at any time, even away from the Games themselves. For instance, at the 1912 Stockholm Games, American champion Jim Thorpe had his pentathlon and decathlon gold medals taken away when it was found he had once been paid a small sum for playing baseball.

American athlete, Jim Thorpe, takes the high jump at the 1912 Games.

▶ Modern Olympic athletes can be professional. American basketball player and Olympic medalist Kobe Bryant is a multimillionaire.

In 1936, the Swiss and Austrian teams refused to attend the Winter Games because anyone who had ever earned money as a ski teacher was banned from taking part.

Time for Change

By the 1970s, it was clear that the rules were outdated and unfair. Athletes from communist countries were training full-time, supported by their governments, and American athletes were being given university scholarships. These competitors were still called amateurs but were really professionals. In 1988, the IOC started to phase out the amateur rule and Olympic stars could now be paid to train. They began to earn money from sponsorship (publicity) deals.

Amazing Olympics

In 1983, the medals that U.S. athlete Jim Thorpe had won at the 1912 Olympics were eventually restored to his family, 30 years after his death.

Olympic Facts and Stats

Athletes at the ancient Olympics were supported financially throughout their training and could become very rich through gifts of food or money from their city-state back home.

Boxing is the only Olympic sport that still does not allow professionals.

The wealthiest athletes in the modern Summer Games are the U.S. basketball team.

The wealthiest Winter Olympic athletes are top U.S. snowboarder Shaun White and South Korean figure skater Kim Yu-na. Both earn more than $8 million a year from sports.

The 1981 movie *Chariots of Fire* showed how snobbery and racism played a part in the early Olympics, when training to win was regarded as shameful and low class.

POLITICS WINS

International politics—arguments between different countries—have caused many disputes centered on the Olympic Games. It is one way of getting global publicity for political views.

Politics were strongly linked to the Olympics in 1936, when they were held in Berlin, Germany. Nazi leader Adolf Hitler tried to use the Games to showcase his Nazi ideas. He thought that the Olympics were ideal for proving that Aryans—white-skinned Christian Germans—were superior to other humans. He was proved spectacularly wrong as the world cheered on African-American Jesse Owens to four track and field gold medals during the Games.

△ Hitler tried to use the 1936 Games to prove Aryan superiority.

The Cold War

From the 1950s through to the 1980s, there was great tension between the communist Soviet Union and its allies and the democratic countries of Western Europe and the United States. It was called the Cold War—the countries didn't actually fight, but they tried to beat each other in every other way they could, especially in sports. At different times both sides boycotted the Games, and in 1956, there was conflict for real, caused by the Soviet Union invading Hungary.

◄ Jesse Owens won four gold medals at the Berlin Olympics, much to Adolf Hitler's fury.

An Olympic water-polo game between Hungary and the Soviet Union became a mass fight and was nicknamed the "blood in the water" game.

Apartheid

In 1964, South Africa was banned from the Olympics because of its racist Apartheid government policy, which segregated (separated) black and white South Africans in different schools, jobs, towns, and also in sports teams. Eventually South Africa canceled its apartheid laws and returned to the Olympics in 1992. In the meantime, its top athletes had to change countries if they wanted to compete. Runner Zola Budd did this in 1984, taking British nationality to run the women's 3,000-meter race, but she failed to win after colliding with another athlete.

▷ U.S. athlete Mary Decker fell after a collision with Zola Budd during the 3,000-meter race in 1984.

Olympic Facts and Stats

1956 The first modern Olympic boycott, when Arab countries withdrew from the Summer Olympics in protest against Israeli actions.

1976 African countries boycotted the Summer Games in protest against New Zealand, who had permitted their rugby team to tour South Africa.

1980 The United States boycotted the Moscow Games in protest against the Soviet Union's invasion of Afghanistan.

1984 The Soviets boycotted the Los Angeles Games as revenge for 1980.

From the 1960s onward, the Olympics began to get worldwide TV coverage, and political protests at the Olympics became international news.

During the 1968 Mexico Games, two African-American medalists made a "black power salute" on the winners' podium. Tommie Smith and John Carlos were showing their support for the struggle for black equality that was then a big political issue in the United States. The Australian silver medalist Peter Norman supported them. The two African-American sprinters were booed by the crowd, banned from the Games, and sent home.

Terror in Munich

In 1972, politics turned to violent tragedy at the Munich Summer Games when Palestinian terrorists broke into the Olympic Village and took members of the Israeli team hostage. Eleven team members, five terrorists, and a policeman were killed in a shoot-out. From then on, security became much tighter at sports events around the world.

▽ An armed German policeman, dressed as an athlete, stands around the corner from a balcony of a dormitory where members of the Black September terrorist group had earlier captured and were then holding a group of Israeli athletes hostage, in Munich, Germany, on September 5, 1972.

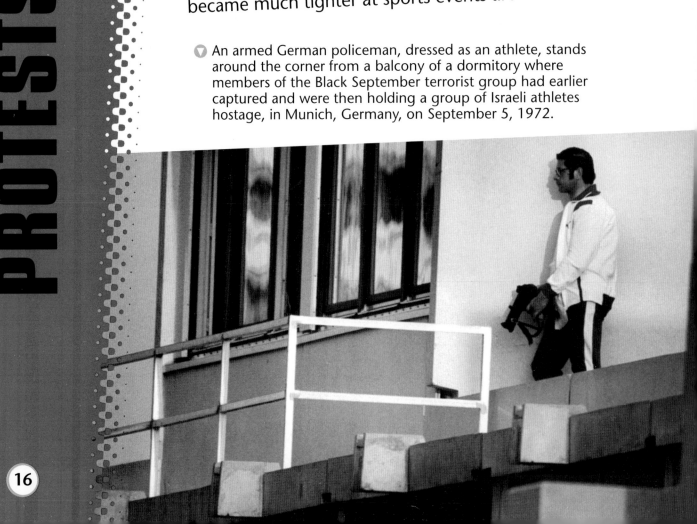

▶ A protestor is restrained by Chinese police at the Beijing Olympics.

Political Protests

When the IOC chooses a country to host the Games, the politics of the host country can cause rows. When China held the Games in 2008, many people protested against the Chinese government's record on human rights. The Olympic torch, a symbol of the Games, was taken on a worldwide journey before the event, but the procession was repeatedly disrupted by anti-Chinese protestors who tried to grab the torch as it went by.

Olympic Facts and Stats

1936 At the Berlin Games, German athletes made the Nazi salute but none of them were banned.

2006 When Australian Peter Norman died in 2006, the two black athletes he had supported in their protest in 1968 helped carry the coffin at his funeral.

2008 At the Beijing Games, banners, T-shirts, and flags supporting Tibet were banned.

2012 After the torch journey was repeatedly hijacked by protestors in the run up to the Beijing Games, there will be no worldwide torch trip before the 2012 London Games. Instead the flame will be carried around the UK.

BRIBES FOR VOTES

Members of the International Olympic Committee vote to decide who will host the Olympic Games. In the 1990s, a big scandal broke when it turned out that some members had secretly been taking bribes for their votes.

Amazing Olympics

The Salt Lake City Olympic Organizing Committee paid $1,000 a month to an IOC member's daughter, to secure his vote.

Cities who want to host an Olympic Games enter a bid to the IOC, explaining their plans. The members look at the bids before they vote and they used to visit the host countries for themselves. In 1998, an anonymous tip-off to a journalist led to an investigation proving that some IOC members had taken bribes from the Organizing Committee of the Salt Lake City Winter Games due to take place in 2002. The bribes included gifts, free vacations, and even jobs and college education for members' families.

Cleaning Up Their Act

It's thought that other cities probably bribed IOC members as well. For the cities that host an Olympic Games, there is worldwide publicity and thousands of new visitors. After the scandal in 1998, the IOC set much stricter rules for its members, forbidding them from visiting any bidders or taking any gifts.

The headquarters of the IOC in Lausanne, Switzerland.

Crowds celebrated after London was awarded the 2012 Olympic Games.

Match Fixing

Bribery may have spread into the Games themselves, too. At the 1988 Seoul Games in South Korea, American boxer Roy Jones lost to South Korean boxer Park Si-hun in a welterweight gold medal contest, even though the American dominated the match and seemed the clear winner. Investigating journalists later discovered that a South Korean millionaire had bribed the boxing judges. One of the judges later admitted he had faked his scoring of the bout.

U.S. boxer Roy Jones was robbed of his 1988 victory due to bribery of the judges.

Olympic Facts and Stats

1976 The Montreal Olympic Games cost so much that the city did not pay off the bill until 1993. After that financial disaster, very few cities wanted to bid for the next few Games.

1984 The Los Angeles Games were so well organized that the city made a good profit. After its success more cities began to bid for the Olympics again.

DOPING TO WIN

Drug-cheating, or "doping," has caused some of the biggest scandals in Olympic history. Drugs are illegal because they can improve an athlete's performance. Cheating athletes are banned from future competitions and stripped of any medals.

The IOC didn't begin to outlaw drug-taking until 1967. Before that athletes were allowed to take whatever they liked to help them compete. For instance, American Thomas Hicks, winner of the 1904 marathon, drank a mixture of strychnine and brandy during the race. Today there are several different types of illegal drug. Some, such as steroids, build up an athlete's muscles. Others help the athlete to cope with stress or the pain of injury. These drugs can have dangerous side effects, including damage to the heart or liver, or health problems later in life.

🔻 Many East German athletes, including multi medal-winning swimmer Kornelia Ender (below), were regularly given steroids by their coaches, usually without their knowledge.

Athletes' blood and urine samples are tested in a lab for traces of illegal drugs.

Drug-Testing

In 1972, the IOC brought in drug-testing to catch cheaters, but crooked doctors and athletics trainers soon began to find ways of faking an athlete's test results or "masking" them— using chemicals to hide traces of performance-enhancing drugs in an athlete's body. This battle between the drug-testers and the drug-taking cheaters is still going on. Testing is done both before and during the Olympic Games, on urine or blood samples taken from the competitors. Occasionally samples have been mixed up, badly tested, or even tampered with, and so drug-cheating accusations usually end up being challenged by lawyers and often take years to sort out.

Amazing Olympics

Before and during the 2012 London Summer Olympics, 5,000 drug tests on athletes are planned, with a further 1,200 for the London Paralympics.

Olympic Facts and Stats

1920 Before the 100-meter race, American athletes drank a mixture of sherry and raw eggs. They won gold and silver medals.

1960 Knut Enemark, a Danish cyclist, collapsed and died during the 100-kilometer race. He had taken a performance-enhancing drug before the event.

2008 At the Beijing Olympics there were 15 positive drug tests during the Games, including positive results for six horses competing in the riding events. A new test developed after the event was used on stored urine samples from athletes and detected six more cheaters.

The list of banned substances for Olympic competitors includes cold and headache remedies.

CAUGHT

The IOC set up the World Anti-Doping Agency in 1999 to test athletes for illegal drug-taking. Competitors have been caught taking illegal drugs in the Summer, Winter, and Paralympic Games.

At the Seoul Olympics in 1988, Ben Johnson of Canada set a world record to win the 100 meters, but became a world-famous cheater when he was stripped of his medal for taking steroids. At first he claimed that his drink had been drugged, but eventually he admitted what he had done. After serving a ban, he began to race again in 1991 but tested positive once again and was banned for life from athletics.

Trouble in the United States

In the 2000s several top-flight U.S. athletes admitted taking performance-enhancing drugs. This followed a police investigation into a San Francisco science laboratory run by Victor Conte, who turned out to be the head of a big drugs ring. The drug-taking cheaters included Olympic gold medal track stars Justin Gatlin, Tim Montgomery, and Marion Jones, who was stripped of the five gold medals she won at the 2000 Sydney Olympics.

Ben Johnson, fastest man on the track, on steroids.

Amazing Olympics

A number of Olympic medals from the 1970s to the 1990s might have been won as a result of drug-cheating, but nobody knows which ones for sure.

East German Athletes

An East German drugs scandal was revealed when secret files came to light in the 1990s after the end of communist rule. Young athletes reported that they were regularly given steroids without their knowledge or their parents' permission. The drug-taking largely escaped detection because one of the medical team for the athletes, Manfred Hoppner, was able to pass on secret information on any new tests because he served on international drugs committees. One of the victims was shot-putter Heidi Krieger, who eventually had to undergo a sex-change operation as a result of the steroids she was given without her knowledge.

▶ East German athlete Heidi Krieger was effectively turned into a man by the steroids she was given.

Olympic Facts and Stats

1968 Swedish athlete Hans-Gunnar Liljenwall was the first athlete to be disqualified for drug-taking after he drank two pints of beer to steady his nerves before his pentathlon event.

1969–89 The coaches and doctors for athletes in East Germany regularly experimented with programs of drugs on the unwitting athletes to improve their performances.

2002 Austrian cross-country skiers were caught cheating at the Salt Lake City Winter Games when a cleaner found drug-taking equipment in their room.

Some Olympic athletes have tried unusual ways of cheating to get onto the medalist's podium.

In 1904, just a few years after the modern Olympics began, American Fred Lorz won the marathon despite extreme heat and dusty roads. It turned out that he had hitched a ride in his trainer's car part of the way through the race. He was about to be awarded the medal when he came clean and told officials he had been given a ride. Years later, at the 1972 Munich Games, a runner joined the marathon late in the race and ran into the stadium as the winner, before being caught by security guards.

Fencing Cheater

At the Montreal Games in 1976, Soviet fencer Boris Onishchenko was doing unusually well when his opponent complained and judges investigated. When a fencing épée (sword) touches an opponent, it registers an electrical signal that scores a "hit." Onishchenko's épée had a secret button that, when pushed, registered a hit, even though Onishchenko hadn't touched his opponent. The Soviet fencing team were thrown out of the Games.

🔻 Marathon runners at the 1904 Olympics in St. Louis, Missouri.

Skating Scandal

In the run-up to the 1994 Lillehammer Winter Games, American figure skater Nancy Kerrigan was attacked by a man who tried to break her leg, though he only bruised it. It was eventually proved that Kerrigan's American rival, Tonya Harding, was involved in the crime. Harding's ex-husband had ordered the attack, but Harding knew all about it. While the investigation went on, Kerrigan and Harding competed in the Olympics. Kerrigan won a silver medal but Harding only came eighth, and faced criminal charges for trying to sabotage her opponent's chances.

Amazing Olympics

There have been several judging scandals at the Olympics, when judges have been accused of cheating to favor their own countries.

Rival American skaters, Nancy Kerrigan (top) and Tonya Harding (bottom).

Olympic Facts and Stats

1984 Madeline de Jesus of Puerto Rico secretly took her injured twin sister's place in a relay heat.

1992 A banned athlete was thrown out of the Olympics after he entered the marathon under a false name. He started the race anyway, and ran for a while before disappearing into the crowd.

1994 The Olympic skating event that featured Nancy Kerrigan and Tonya Harding drew one of the biggest TV audiences in American history because of the scandal. There has even been an opera written about it.

2002 At the Salt Lake City Winter Games, a French figure-skating judge admitted cheating when scoring.

Some Olympic controversies have been caused by medical questions. These have provided complicated problems for officials trying to write fair rules.

Athletes taking part in the Paralympics have their disability classified, which means they are put into groups to compete against other athletes with a similar level of disability. This has led to a few people cheating by exaggerating their disability to get into a group they know they can win. The worst case of faking was at the Sydney Olympics in 2000, when Spain won gold with a basketball team that was supposed to be mentally disabled. In fact, the athletes faked their disability for money. Sadly their actions led to all competitions for mentally disabled people being dropped from the Paralympics.

⬀ Dora Ratjen, the German high-jumper, was in fact a man named Horst.

Gender Troubles

Occasionally, female Olympic athletes have been suspected of being men, because of the way they look. Men are physically stronger than women and would have an unfair advantage in a sports competition. On rare occasions men have entered the Olympics pretending to be women, but more commonly people with intersex characteristics have been the subject of controversy. Roughly 1 in 1,000 humans are born "intersex," which means they have a mixture of male and female genetics. Athletes' blood samples can be genetically tested by the Olympic authorities, and the rules are currently to judge intersex athletes individually to decide if they can compete.

Amazing Olympics

Transexuals are allowed to compete in the Olympics two years after their operation, if they have changed from male to female.

Stella Walsh

In the early decades of the modern Olympics, there was no genetic testing and no understanding of intersex people, only allegations and suspicion. One famous controversy was in 1936, when 100-meter runner Stella Walsh lost to her rival Helen Stephens and then accused Helen Stephens of being a man. Doctors examined Stephens and confirmed that she was a woman, but many years later, when Stella Walsh died, it was discovered that she was in fact intersex, with mixed gender.

⬥ Stella Walsh, who turned out to have mixed gender.

⬥ Helen Stephens (left), whom Walsh accused of being a man.

Olympic Facts and Stats

During the Paralympics, wheelchair athletes have occasionally found that their wheelchairs have been sabotaged before a race.

1936 German Olympic high-jumper Dora Ratjen turned out to be a man whose real name was Horst Ratjen.

Mentally disabled athletes can currently compete in a program of "Special Olympics" meetings, which are events run by charities that are allowed to use the "Olympics" name.

The Olympic rules covering mentally disabled competitors and intersex athletes are highly controversial and may well be changed in the future.

FUTURE SHOCKS

Here are some issues that may face the Olympics in the future. One thing is for certain: any Olympic scandals will get worldwide publicity because it is the world's biggest and most popular sports event.

Scientists are developing more and more hi-tech equipment to help athletes perform better, but only athletes from wealthy nations can afford to use it, which makes competition unfair. It's been called "technological doping" because it gives competitors an advantage in the same way as performance-enhancing drugs.

Amazing Olympics

The IOC is now storing blood samples from Olympic athletes for eight years, in case tests are invented in the near future that might show up drug-cheating methods.

The "Fastskin"

In the 2008 Beijing Olympics, there was controversy when many swimming records were broken by swimmers wearing a new and expensive hi-tech costume, the Speedo "Fastskin," which was designed with help from NASA space experts. The costume squeezed swimmers into a more aerodynamic shape so they could travel faster through water. It was declared legal to wear but has since been banned.

◄ Michael Phelps in a "Fastskin." This type of swimsuit is so tight, it takes about 30 minutes to get one on.

Gene Doping

In the future it may be possible to genetically change (alter the body cells) of athletes to help them build bigger muscles or make more oxygen in their blood, so they can perform better. This idea is called "gene doping." It would be very hard to detect. The technology for it has been developed to treat medical conditions, but no one has admitted to using it on an athlete yet. One type of gene therapy drug, called repoxygen, helps someone create more oxygen in the blood, enabling muscles to work harder for longer.

Cheaters who take drugs are always trying to find new ways to evade dope tests, using the latest science to improve their performance.

Green Issues

A big issue facing the Olympics is how much environmental damage it causes. Olympic host cities are trying to design Olympic sites and transportation that cause the least environmental damage and can be reused in the future. Green campaigners say not enough has been done yet to make the Olympics more environmentally friendly.

The 2012 London Olympic site is designed to be environmentally friendly.

Olympic Facts and Stats

2010 The Vancouver Games tried to be the greenest yet. The Olympic Villages were heated with energy generated from sewage.

A typical Summer Games carbon footprint has been calculated at 3.4 million tons of carbon—the equivalent of the amount of carbon 300,000 people make a year.

The IOC has declared that the Olympics must promote three things—sports, culture (arts), and caring for the environment.

GLOSSARY

Amateur athlete Someone who doesn't earn money from their sport, which is not their fulltime job.

Anabolic steroids Drugs used to increase muscle strength. They can also alter the body's hormone balance, gradually turning women into men, with much more body hair, a deep voice, and internal damage to the body.

Apartheid The segregation (separation) of black and white people in South Africa during part of the twentieth century. The policy led to South Africa being banned from the Olympics.

Boycott Refusing to take part in something as a protest. Countries sometimes refuse to take part in the Olympics as a protest against the politics of another nation involved in the Games.

Carbon footprint The amount of carbon made by an activity. A measure of pollution caused.

Cold War A period between the 1950s and 1980s when there was suspicion and hostility between communist countries of the Soviet Union and Western democratic countries of the Americas and Europe.

Intersex A human with a mixture of male and female genetics.

IOC International Olympic Committee, the organization that runs the Olympic Games. It is headed by the President of the IOC.

Marathon A long-distance running race that takes place through the streets of the host city during the Summer Olympics.

Nazi A member of the National Socialist German Workers, which came to power in Germany in 1933 under the leadership of Adolf Hitler.

Olympia The site of the first Olympics, held in Ancient Greece in 776 B.C.E.

Olympiad An Olympic event held every four years.

Olympic bid A proposal put forward by a city in order to win the right to host the Olympic Games.

Olympic charter A set of rules stating how the Games will be run.

Olympic motto "*Citius, Altius, Fortius,*" meaning "higher, faster, stronger."

Olympic oath A promise made by athletes and judges to abide by the rules and honor the values and spirit of the Olympic Games.

Olympic rings The logo of the Olympic Games, made up of five rings representing the five continents from which the athletes are drawn, on a white background symbolizing peace.

Olympic torch A flame brought from Olympia in Greece to the Olympic stadium in the host city. It burns throughout the Games.

Olympic Village Accommodation built for the athletes taking part in the Games.

Pagan The follower of a religion that worships nature.

Paralympics Olympics held every four years for athletes with disabilities.

Performance-enhancing drugs Drugs taken to make an athlete perform better (also called "doping").

Polis Ancient Greek city-states that competed with one another in the ancient Olympics.

Professional athlete Someone whose sport is their full-time job, from which they earn money.

Track and field event An event that takes place on the athletic running track, or in the center of the running track, such as long jump or javelin-throwing.

World Anti-Doping Agency Set up by the International Olympic Committee to test athletes for illegal drug-taking. WADA for short.

Youth Olympics Summer and Winter Olympic Games held every four years for athletes between 14 and 18 years old.

Zeus Greek god honored by the ancient Greeks at the Olympic Games.

Modern Summer Olympic Games Timeline

1896 Athens, Greece

1900 Paris, France

1904 St. Louis, Missouri

1908 London, UK

1912 Stockholm, Sweden

1916 Not held because of World War I

1920 Antwerp, Belgium

1924 Paris, France

1928 Amsterdam (Netherlands)

1932 Los Angeles, California

1936 Berlin, Germany

1940 Canceled because of World War II

1944 Canceled because of World War II

1948 London, UK

1952 Helsinki, Finland

1956 Melbourne, Australia

1960 Rome, Italy (First Paralympic Summer Games also held)

1964 Tokyo, Japan

1968 Mexico City, Mexico

1972 Munich (West Germany)

1976 Montreal, Canada

1980 Moscow, USSR

1984 Los Angeles, California

1988 Seoul, South Korea

1992 Barcelona, Spain

1996 Atlanta, Georgia

2000 Sydney, Australia

2004 Athens, Greece

2008 Beijing, China

2012 London, UK

2016 Rio De Janeiro, Brazil

Winter Olympics Timeline

1924 Chamonix, France

1928 St. Moritz, Switzerland

1932 Lake Placid, New York

1936 Garmisch, Germany

1940 Canceled because of World War II

1944 Canceled because of World War II

1948 St. Moritz, Switzerland

1952 Oslo, Norway

1956 Cortina d'Ampezzo, Italy

1960 Squaw Valley, California

1964 Innsbruck, Austria

1968 Grenoble, France

1972 Sapporo, Japan

1976 Innsbruck, Austria

1976 First Paralympic Winter Games held Ornskoldsvik, Sweden

1980 Lake Placid, New York

1984 Sarajevo, Yugoslavia (now Bosnia)

1988 Calgary, Alberta, Canada

1992 Albertville, France

1994 Lillehammer, Norway

1998 Nagano, Japan

2002 Salt Lake City, Utah

2006 Turin, Italy

2010 Vancouver, British Columbia, Canada

2014 Sochi, Russia

Useful Olympic web sites

www. olympic.org The official web site of the Olympic Movement.

www.www.teamusa.org Official site of the U.S. Olympic Team.

www.london2012.com The official web site of the London Summer Olympics, 2012.

www.paralympics.org The official web site of the Paralympics.

www.enchantedlearning.com/olympics Find out about the history of the ancient Greek Games and print up a game activity book.

INDEX